CREATIVE WAYS TO LOVE & ENCOURAGE HIM

DATING EDITION

ALYSSA BETHKE

with BRITTNI DE LA MORA

Published in Pasadena, CA, by Aloha and Rain. Aloha and Rain titles may be purchased in bulk for educational, business, fundraising, or sales promotional use. For information, please e-mail info@alohaandrain.com.

Unless otherwise noted, Scriptures are taken from the Holy Bible, New International Version®, NIV®. Copyright © 1973, 1978, 1984, 2011 by Biblica, Inc.™ Used by permission of Zondervan. All rights reserved worldwide. www.zondervan.com.

The Library of Congress Cataloging-in-Publication
Data is on file with the Library of Congress
ISBN-13: 978-1-7342746-4-6

TABLE OF CONTENTS

HOW TO GET THE MOST OUT OF THIS BOOK

First off, you rock. By getting these paired books and wanting to go through them with your significant other, you obviously are already dominating at life! We have prayed over this project and believe it can be a fun way to cultivate a healthy relationship and bring back the joy and intimacy that sometimes gets lost amidst everyday activities.

To get the most out of this book, we'd first say lean in. Lean into the ideas, the spontaneity and the parts that stretch you the most. Don't be afraid to just go for it, have fun and create memories. We are firm believers that with these two books, whatever you put into it you will get out of it. Isn't that true with all our relationships as a whole? Also, know that this is just a template. Some things won't fit for your relationship, or you can't do based on certain locations, resources, and other variables. We have tried to make every day as applicable for everyone as possible. So with that being said, feel free to morph it, change it, adapt it and do whatever you need to do to get the most out of it. Because at the end of the day, the goal isn't to follow this book rigidly and *"cross each day off your checklist,"* but rather it's to bring a fresh vibrancy and life back to your relationship.

We are so excited to release this edition for couples who are dating and engaged! We teamed up with another married couple, Rich and Brittni De La Mora for their insight on dating. You will see comments from them throughout the book, we love and appreciate their wisdom and you will too! The next 31 days are going to bring fresh fire and excitement into your relationship. Have fun and keep us updated on social media by hashtagging #31CreativeWays.

JEFF & ALYSSA BETHKE

DAY ONE: FIRST THINGS FIRST

Hands down the best thing you can do for your man is pray for him. I know a lot of times I'm tempted to do something else, something *"better"* or more noticeable. Which doing other things are great and part of pursuing him-hence this book! But prayer needs to be the foundation. I can't tell you how many times I've prayed for Jeff and then have been amazed at how God has moved in his heart. But even more so, I think prayer is what moves my heart to love and pursue him. I've found that when I'm consistently praying for Jeff, I'm way more patient, kind and gentle with him; I find myself cheering him on, being intentional and putting him above myself. A lot of times too, I don't know how to pursue Jeff. What could I do to show him I love him? That I'm thinking of him today? Lately, when I've asked the Lord to show me how to serve and love him, He leads me to do something for Jeff that ends up blessing Jeff that day. God knows our men the best, so why don't we ask Him to show us how to love them?

Brittni's Insight:

It started when my husband and I were dating. I refused to talk to him before I first spoke to God. I did (and still do) this because I wanted to show God that my time spent with Him was my number one priority. I also know that I become a different woman after spending time with God. In my time of prayer, God humbles me and gives me the ability to love my husband more. I have found that when you seek after the God of love, you will become a deliverer of His love.

To avoid any distractions, I would (and still do) put my phone on *"Do Not Disturb"* before going to bed. During my time of prayer, I would pray for my boyfriend and ask God for a word for him. Then after praying, I would send Rich a word of encouragement that was given to me by God Himself.

I did this every day because I wanted him to know that when we were married, he was going to have a wife who believed in God's miracles and promises. I wanted him to rest assured knowing that with me as his wife, I would prayerfully change the atmosphere of our home and God would always be the solid foundation on which we would build our marriage.

This morning, first things first; before calling your boyfriend, first call God. Call Him through prayer and call Him on behalf of your boyfriend. Pray boldly for him and ask God for a word that will encourage and inspire your man to be the best he can be today. Send him a text message or give him a call to let him know the amazing things God has to say to him today. I guarantee that your boyfriend or fiance will be moved by this act of encouragement.

JOURNAL BELOW:

WRITE WHAT YOU LEARNED TODAY, HOW IT WENT AND WHAT MEMORIES WERE MADE

DAY TWO: TELL THE TRUTH

John 8:32 (NLT) says, *"And you will know that truth, and the truth will set you free."*

Brittni's Insight:
One thing I love to do for my husband is speak the word of God over his life. I read the Bible daily, and often I will find a scripture that reminds me of him or a particular obstacle we are facing. What I love about the Bible is every word brings forth truth, hope, correction, and encouragement into our lives. It reminds us that though we may face unpromising circumstances, we serve a God who is full of promises, and His promises have the power to free us from whatever challenges we may face.

When my husband and I were dating, there was a time when he went through many trials and tribulations. At the time, his life reminded me of two people in the Bible-Job and Joseph. My husband is a man of integrity. He practices what he preaches, so for him to be hit with as much warfare as he was hit with was shocking. I remember him asking, in a moment of breakdown, *"Why me? I try to do everything right. I've been celibate for seven years, I seek God daily, I love Him with all of my heart, I serve Him and His people, and I have given up my life for Him."* At that moment, I didn't have a clear answer for him, but the next morning, I searched the Scriptures and texted him the greatest piece of truth I could find.

I said something along these lines, *"Love, I know what you're going through doesn't make sense, but like Job and Joseph, you are going to be a great hero of our faith and every great hero must be tested. The word of God has this to say about your situation in Psalm 105:9 (NLT)..."* Until the time came to fulfill Richard's dreams, the Lord tested Richard's character." And in Job 42:10 (NLT), *"The Lord restored Richard's fortunes. In fact, the Lord gave him twice as much as before."*

I made the scriptures personal by replacing the Joseph and Job's name with my boyfriend's name. When he read that text, it brought him so much hope because that morning the truth set him free, brought him comfort and peace.

The truth carries power. Tell your man the truth today! Pray and ask God to give you Scripture for your boyfriend or fiance. You can also google *"encouraging Scriptures for my boyfriend."* As you read through them, you'll know which one will encourage your man today. Make it personal by adding his name to the Scripture and then text it to him. This gesture will uplift your man today, and he will have a better day because of it. Let us know what Scripture you spoke over your man today on social media by hashtagging #31CreativeWays.

JOURNAL BELOW:

WRITE WHAT YOU LEARNED TODAY, HOW IT WENT AND WHAT MEMORIES WERE MADE

_____

_____

_____

_____

_____

_____

DAY THREE: BUT FIRST, YOU!

Jeff's all time favorite thing is getting his feet massaged. If there is one way I can serve him, it's that. If we're debating over something and we decide to bet on it, if I throw out that I'll massage his feet if I lose, he's all in. If I don't know what to get him for Christmas, I always have lotion and a foot massage to lean back on. It's the best in his book. And if I'm totally honest with you, I have to talk myself into it because GROSS. I mean, I adore my husband, but touching feet isn't on my list of favorite things to do. However, when I see how much Jeff loves it, it gives me joy.

Brittni's Insight:
I am often inspired by the servant hearts many women in the Bible possessed. The other day I was reading about a woman named Abigail in 1 Samuel 25. After her husband Nabal died, David asked her to be his wife. Her response was, *"Here is your maidservant, a servant to wash the feet of the servants of my Lord."* (1 Samuel 25:41-NKJV) I was convicted when I read this verse because this woman counted it all joy to be given the opportunity to serve her husband. I felt as though there have been many opportunities I have overlooked to serve my husband and even complained about some. After reading this scripture, I decided that I want to be intentional about taking on the heart of Abigail. I want to look for ways to serve my husband because I know that in doing so, God will find ways to serve me, and I know my husband will feel at ease as I serve him.

Today, let's take on the heart of a servant. *"Babe, I have things to do today, but first, YOU!"* Ask your boyfriend how you can serve him today. He might ask for you to pack him a lunch for the following day or run an errand for him. Who knows what he will ask for?! The point is, to do what you can to serve him today and to do it joyfully. Tell us how it went on social media #31CreativeWays.

JOURNAL BELOW:

WRITE WHAT YOU LEARNED TODAY, HOW IT
WENT AND WHAT MEMORIES WERE MADE

DAY FOUR:
L.O.L

Brittni's Insight:

Laughter is one of life's greatest medicines. When my husband and I were dating, we would spend hours together on Instagram looking at funny videos. We would laugh together for hours. By the time he had to go home, my cheeks and my stomach hurt from all the laughter. Laughter has always brought us closer together because when you laugh together, you get lost in the moment together. Laughing together always made it feel like we were the only two people in the world.

Proverbs 31:25(NLT) says, *"She laughs without fear of the future."* I love this scripture because it reminds us that we can't laugh and be fearful at the same time. Laughter rids your heart of worry and fear; it is medicine for your soul.

Today, if you have plans to see your boyfriend, laugh together. Put on a good comedy show, play Pictionary, or hashtag #funnyvideos on Instagram and see what comes up. If you won't see your boyfriend today, find something funny on social media or the internet and send it his way. Laughter has a way of bringing added joy and longevity to relationships. So today, L.O.L.

JOURNAL BELOW:

WRITE WHAT YOU LEARNED TODAY, HOW IT
WENT AND WHAT MEMORIES WERE MADE

_____

_____

_____

_____

_____

_____

_____

_____

_____

_____

_____

_____

_____

_____

DAY FIVE: WORSHIP

Brittni's Insight:

Worship is one of my favorite things to do. Every morning, I turn on my favorite worship song and lift my hands to Heaven. I do this because I love God so much and for all that He's done in my life, He is worthy to be worshiped. When I worship God, His presence brings me hope, love, strength, and peace. Worship is the greatest way to usher God's presence into any household because our worship attracts the heart of God.

Matthew 18:20(NIV) says, *"Where two or three are gathered in my name, there I am with them."* This scripture teaches us that when you and your man gather together in worship, God will be with you. Ladies, no matter what happens in your life, so long as God is the center, every little thing is going to be alright. With God at the center of your relationship, you can rest assured that He will strengthen and lead your relationship.

Today, worship with your man! Pick your favorite worship song, start off with a prayer and lift your hands up to God. As you do this, His presence will unify your relationship, bring peace and healing to your hearts, and will refresh your soul. I am so excited to hear how this challenge has grown you and your man! Make sure to post about it on social media with hashtag #31CreativeWays.

JOURNAL BELOW:

WRITE WHAT YOU LEARNED TODAY, HOW IT
WENT AND WHAT MEMORIES WERE MADE

_____

_____

_____

_____

_____

_____

_____

_____

_____

_____

_____

_____

_____

_____

DAY SIX:
LET IT GO

"Love keeps no record of wrongs."
1 Corinthians 13:5(NIV)

Brittni's Insight:

It is unfortunate to admit that I used to be a living product of my mistakes. I know first-hand the danger of keeping record of wrongs. I grew up in a household full of hurt and pain. When one would make a mistake, it was rarely forgotten. Our mistakes were continuously thrown into our faces. This was detrimental to my emotional health. I became afraid to make decisions because I was in fear that I would make the wrong one and get ridiculed for it.

I didn't learn until later in life that mistakes are a blessing from God. It is through my mistakes that I have learned more about myself and life than when I do something right.

In relationships, mistakes will be made, and accidents will happen; that is inevitable. However, it is how we process the mistakes with our partner that often becomes the make or break of the scenario. If you want to be for the long haul with your partner, then you need to make him feel safe coming to you. He shouldn't feel like he is going to get ridiculed, or that you're going to *"forgive, but never forget."*

Remember, it isn't impossible to have a prosperous future with your partner if you choose to live in the past. Therefore, we need to destroy all record of wrongs by letting go of our hurts and offenses; because this is what love does. Love uplifts, love encourages, love brings safety, love brings hope, and love never gives up (see 1 Corinthians 13:4-8 NIV).

Today, talk to your boyfriend about forgiveness. Is there something you need forgiveness for? Ask for it. Is there something you need to forgive him for? Then do it. If the slate between the two of you is clear, then have a conversation about the power of forgiveness and if there is anyone you need to forgive. Today is the day to let it go.

JOURNAL BELOW:

WRITE WHAT YOU LEARNED TODAY, HOW IT
WENT AND WHAT MEMORIES WERE MADE

_____

_____

_____

_____

_____

_____

_____

_____

_____

_____

_____

_____

_____

DAY SEVEN: ENTER HIS WORLD

Brittni's Insight:

Ladies, dating is the perfect time to get to know your man. This season of life is meant to be fun. When my husband and I were dating, I did something that I have never admitted to anyone until now. I googled *"Questions to ask a man while dating."* The reason I did this was that getting to know my man was important to me and I wanted to make sure that I was asking all the right questions, so I sought out wisdom... from Google.

I would memorize as many questions as I could and our dates we would pretty much play, *"21 Questions."* It's important that you learn as much as you can about your man because after all, you might get to spend the rest of your life with him. Eeeek! How exciting! It's also important because the more you know about your man, the better the woman you can be for him. If you know what he loves, then you can bring those kinds of things into his life. For example, when my husband and I first started dating, he told me his favorite meal was chicken piccata, and his favorite fruit was raspberry. When his birthday rolled around, I invited him to my apartment for dinner. I surprised him with homemade chicken piccata and a homemade vanilla cake with a raspberry filling. I was petrified because I had never made chicken piccata before but I wanted to impress my man, so I did it anyway.

I spoke my husband's language back then with this creative act of love. Now it's your turn. What is something your boyfriend loves that would make him think, *"Wow! My girl gets me!"*? It may be a sport, a certain genre of movie, a book that he's currently reading, working out, cooking, gardening, music, cars, etc. Today (or sometime this week) do that hobby with him. Go see that movie he's been dying to see with him in the theatre, go watch his softball game and cheer him on, pick up a copy of the book he's reading and read it together, listen to him play guitar, ask him to show you something about cars, or cook him his favorite meal. Whatever you decide to do, make sure you speak HIS language this week.

JOURNAL BELOW:

WRITE WHAT YOU LEARNED TODAY, HOW IT
WENT AND WHAT MEMORIES WERE MADE

DAY EIGHT: BREAKFAST IS THE MOST IMPORTANT MEAL OF THE DAY

About six months into dating Jeff, he got a new job and had to travel a lot. I MEAN A LOT. Like every week. Some trips he would land in Seattle at 2 pm and have to fly back out at 5 pm that same night. To say it was hard for me is an understatement! I mean, I loved that he was loving what he was doing and was so filled up but man, I missed my guy.

For one of his trips, I got to drive him to the airport early that morning because I didn't have work that day. I hadn't seen him much, so we decided we'd stop at the nearest Starbucks by the airport for a quick coffee date before he flew out. Obviously, Starbucks has coffee (mmmm coffee) and pastries, but I wanted to make it a special little coffee break for us, so I whipped up some cream cheese peach muffins for Jeff. 1. Because he loves cream cheese. 2. Because he loves anything peach. 3. Because I straight up love muffins. I put them in a basket with napkins and a note and brought them into Starbucks with us.

Looking back now that I'm married and know my husband, that was just a little appetizer for him, maybe even an appetizer to the appetizer! A muffin is just a snack to Jeff; he needs the full meal deal. Eggs, potatoes, toast. Regardless, he loved those muffins, but I think even more so, he loved that I thought of him and made something that had his favorites in it. And really, it didn't take that much of an effort on my part.

Today, think of a fun breakfast treat that your man would enjoy (muffins, cinnamon rolls, donuts, bagels, etc.). Meet up with him tomorrow morning and share your treat together. If that's not possible, then leave it where he'll find it in the morning (or take it to his work) with a cute little note just saying you were thinking of him and you hope he has a great day.

JOURNAL BELOW:

WRITE WHAT YOU LEARNED TODAY, HOW IT
WENT AND WHAT MEMORIES WERE MADE

DAY NINE: COMPLIMENTS BRING CONFIDENCE

Words are powerful. They can either build up or tear down. Words can either destroy a relationship or make it flourish. Jeff is so good about telling me every day that he loves me and is thankful for me. He constantly tells me that I'm beautiful and a wonderful wife and mom. Can I be honest with you? Most of the time, especially lately, I sure don't feel beautiful. I probably already botched up being a wonderful wife and mom that day by a comment I made or by being impatient or selfish. But when Jeff looks me in the eyes and speaks those words over me, I start to believe them instead of getting bogged down by the lies I can so easily believe about myself. And that gives me life. It gives me hope. It helps me to see myself the way God sees me, and it helps me to be a better wife and mom. Insecurities fly out the door. Feelings of being overwhelmed or anxious are exchanged for the courage to do the task God's given me.

It can be easy to not speak life into our men because we're too busy, but it is important! So today, look your man in the eyes and tell him how thankful you are for him and at least one thing that you love about him. If you don't have the opportunity to see him today, then call him to compliment him. Think of something specific like, *"I admire your work ethic, you inspire me to be better and to do better"* or *"I love how you listen to people and make them feel heard."* When you compliment your man, you'll bring confidence to your man!

JOURNAL BELOW:

WRITE WHAT YOU LEARNED TODAY, HOW IT
WENT AND WHAT MEMORIES WERE MADE

DAY TEN:
TEN THINGS
I LOVE
ABOUT YOU

A few weeks ago I was praying for Jeff and had asked the Lord to show me how I could encourage him that day. It had been a week after I had given birth to our son Kannon, so I felt pretty tapped out and not able to do much for Jeff. I was getting ready in our bathroom and saw our dry erase marker in a basket. You never know when you need to write a little note on your bathroom mirror! So I grabbed that bad boy and wrote out ten things I loved about Jeff on his side of the mirror. It took me probably 5 minutes. It wasn't pretty or designed or super thought out. It was just a little overflow of my heart letting him know that I love him, see him and am thankful for all he does. Later that day, I was sitting on our couch, when he came out and told me how much that list meant to him. It made his day! It was just a small gesture that made all the difference that day.

Today, write out ten things that you love and appreciate about your man and give it to him the next time you see him.

JOURNAL BELOW:

WRITE WHAT YOU LEARNED TODAY, HOW IT WENT AND WHAT MEMORIES WERE MADE

_____

_____

_____

_____

DAY ELEVEN: HOW HE'S GROWN

Life can be discouraging at times, and we can get bogged down by thinking of all the things we aren't doing right, what we need to do differently, what we need to change or how we failed in a particular task or moment. I think too; often it's harder to see what God is doing in us or the ways we've grown. But God is always at work in our lives, and we are always growing if we're seeking Him. There is always fruit, even if it's just a seed.

When you're doing life with someone, it's so important to point out areas you see them growing in because often they don't see it themselves. There is nothing like hearing someone, especially someone close to you, tell you that you're doing an awesome job in this area or how you've become more patient, gentle or kind in this way. It's so encouraging and gives you hope that you are growing, even though you're not perfect and still have room to change.

Today, tell your man at least one area that you've seen him grow in lately and how proud you are of him. If you're not sure what that is, spend some time praying and thinking of the past couple of weeks. When you spend time praying for your man, you're more attuned to what God is doing in his life.

*Note: When you tell him how he's grown today, don't tell him how bad he was at something before! Just mention how you've seen him be a certain way lately and how proud you are of him.

Brittni's Insight:

For instance, *"Love, I have noticed you've been extremely patient. Lately, it seems like nothing can bring you down. I love that about you."* Or, *"Babe, I've noticed you have been bolder in your faith lately! The way you trust God and encourage others inspires me."*

49

JOURNAL BELOW:

WRITE WHAT YOU LEARNED TODAY, HOW IT
WENT AND WHAT MEMORIES WERE MADE

DAY TWELVE: FAITH COMES BY HEARING

"So then faith comes by hearing and hearing,
and hearing the word of God."
Romans 10:17(NKJV)

Brittni's Insight:

Over the years, I've learned one of the greatest ways to activate someone's faith is to pray for them. Not in the privacy of your bedroom when they can't hear you, but while you are with them. Romans 10:17 says, *"faith comes by hearing"* so through prayer you possess the power to activate your man's faith.

When we were dating, Rich prepared an incredible message on spiritual warfare to preach to the young adult ministry we lead. That Friday night, just hours before it was time to preach he wanted to throw the towel in. He was physically and emotionally drained from the long week he had and didn't think he had any more energy left to preach. I looked him in the eyes and said, *"Love, God called you for such a time as this. You can't give up now. Many lives are going to be saved and radically changed tonight."* Then I began to pray that God would strengthen him and give him rest for his soul. As I prayed for him, there was a shift in his heart. His faith to believe in the miraculous was activated. When he preached that night the altar was packed with people wanting to give their lives to the Lord. One prayer changed the course of what could have been a disappointment and turned it into a night of success.

Ladies, if you'll see your man today, confidently pray for him. If you won't see him, then give him a call and tell him you'd like to pray for him while on the phone with him. Your prayer has the power to uplift and encourages your man. He will also appreciate you bringing God into the center of your relationship.

JOURNAL BELOW:

WRITE WHAT YOU LEARNED TODAY, HOW IT
WENT AND WHAT MEMORIES WERE MADE

_____

_____

_____

_____

_____

_____

_____

_____

_____

_____

_____

_____

_____

DAY THIRTEEN: THE LITTLE THINGS

Last week we celebrated Mother's Day. I had wanted eyelash extensions FOREVER, so I finally got them. Because who has time to put on make-up with a toddler and newborn!? I told Jeff that was my Mother's Day gift. All that to say, I wasn't expecting anything on Mother's Day, I just wanted to be with my family and celebrate my mom. After we had a special breakfast and played in the yard, both the kids fell asleep (oh how I cherish you sweet nap time), so I told Jeff I was going to take a bath and lay down for a bit. While I was rocking Kins asleep in her room, Jeff went ahead and got my bath ready. He filled it with bath salts and bubble bath, lit a candle, put on music, grabbed my book and wrote a little note that said: *"I LOVE YOU."* When I came out of Kinsley's room, I smelled the bath salts and went into the bathroom amazed. Talk about an amazing husband! How thoughtful was he!? You know the funny thing though? Amidst all that wonderfulness, my favorite part was the little note that said: *"I LOVE YOU."* I know I'm a words person. I feel the most loved by the written word. And I'll take it in any form-texts, emails, cards. But there was something just so sweet about seeing Jeff's handwriting on that bright blue card in bold font. I still have it hanging up in my bathroom mirror.

Little surprises that say, *"Hey, I'm thinking of you,"* are always sweet and special. It's such a good feeling to know that someone has you in his or her mind. And it can be the littlest thing! Today, put a little something in his car as a sweet surprise. It could be a little note that says *"I LOVE YOU,"* your picture on his dashboard or his favorite candy bar. Anything that says you're thinking of him.

JOURNAL BELOW:

WRITE WHAT YOU LEARNED TODAY, HOW IT
WENT AND WHAT MEMORIES WERE MADE

_____

_____

_____

_____

_____

_____

_____

_____

_____

_____

_____

_____

_____

_____

DAY FOURTEEN: MAKE IT KNOWN

If you're on Facebook or Instagram, I'm sure you've seen ladies post about their men and use #MCM (Man Crush Monday). Although I always forget to post about Jeff on Mondays just like I always forget to do a #TBT (Throwback Thursday) until Friday-I love this concept!

Brittni's Insight:
In a world that is well able to tell our men everything that they aren't and everything that they can't do, we need to be the type of women who encourage our men and speak life into them. Let's bring them confidence by making it known we are proud of our men.

I love what the Bible teaches us in Proverbs 15:4 (MSG), *"Kind words heal and help; cutting words wound a maim."*

This scripture teaches us that our kind words matter. They both heal and help. Can I remind you that one kind word can help the position of your man's heart? One kind word can help bring him from a place of weakness and into a place of strength.

So today, let's do just that! Let's bring our men into a place of strength by making known that he is your man. Post a Facebook or Instagram post about how thankful you are for your man. Use #31creativeways so we can all see it and cheer each other on as women who honor their men!

JOURNAL BELOW:

WRITE WHAT YOU LEARNED TODAY, HOW IT
WENT AND WHAT MEMORIES WERE MADE

DAY FIFTEEN: MY FAVORITE LOVE STORY

One of my favorite questions to ask a couple is how they met or when did they know that was the person they wanted to spend the rest of their lives with. The best is hearing the couple go back and forth, playing off of each other and hearing them recount their story. As they talk, you can still see the sparkle in their eye, and by the end of the story, it's like they are closer in some way. They are enjoying one another more than when they sat down because they're reminded of how sweet their story is and how much they love each other.

Brittni's Insight:

Bring a little sparkle back today by posting a photo of you and your man on social media and share your favorite love story (Yours of course) in the caption. Talk about how you met and how you knew he was the one. Hashtag #31CreativeWays so we call read your love story! If you don't have social media, then write a note to your guy telling him your meeting story and when you started to fall for him. It can be a long letter or just a simple note to remind him of your beginnings.

JOURNAL BELOW:

WRITE WHAT YOU LEARNED TODAY, HOW IT WENT AND WHAT MEMORIES WERE MADE

DAY SIXTEEN: ATTITUDE OF GRATITUDE

Is it really easy to complain and think of all the things you'd like to be different right? Unfortunately, this is easy to do when it comes to your man. There have been times when I let my mind wander and go down rabbit trails of how I'd like Jeff to be different. Or rather, things I'd like for him to do differently. How he can change. Areas he needs to grow in. Things I dislike; areas I get frustrated or irritated by. Yuck! Even just writing this out, I feel trapped and down.

It's good to see areas someone can grow in, to pray for them and encourage them to be the best version of themselves that they can be. It's never good to get into a pit of ungratefulness and complaining. It's toxic and not only will it bring you down, but it will also bring down the relationship. Cultivating a heart of thankfulness is so vital in life, as well as in a relationship. Thinking of how thankful you are for your man and listing out ways that you're thankful for him is so important.

Today's task isn't so much for him, but for you. Fostering a thankful heart for him will naturally overflow into your relationship and will affect how you see him. This will impact him because you'll become more joy-filled, grateful and kind, instead of complaining, nagging or harboring bitterness.

Brittni's Insight:

Today list out ways that you are thankful for him. It can be the littlest thing to the biggest thing. Throughout the day, text him one-by-one the reasons you are thankful for him. Keep this list in the pages we've provided and read it from time to time as a reminder to you that you have many reasons to be thankful for your man. If you're feeling bold enough to let us all know why you're thankful for your man, post your list on social media and hashtag #31CreativeWays.

JOURNAL BELOW:

WRITE WHAT YOU LEARNED TODAY, HOW IT
WENT AND WHAT MEMORIES WERE MADE

_____

_____

_____

_____

_____

_____

_____

_____

_____

_____

_____

_____

_____

_____

DAY SEVENTEEN: CANDY CRUSH

When Jeff and I first started dating, it was long distance. He was in Oregon going to college, and I was across the Pacific Ocean in Hawaii doing an internship at a church. Although long distance has it pits-like, you're not together! But one good thing is it forces you to get creative. Like really creative. I mean, when you can't hang out, go on dates or see each other at church, you're forced to find ways to show each other that you care other than the phone.

One Valentine's Day I decided to make Jeff a candy gram. I went to the store and bought as many different candy bars as I could find. Then I put a bunch of construction paper together like a book and wrote him a love letter using the candy bars as fill in words. Next thing I know, I'm getting a telephone call with Jeff on the other end, munching on a candy bar, proclaiming how awesome my candy gram was! HE LOVED IT.

Today, go to the grocery store or gas station and pick up some candy bars to make your own candy gram for your man. Some good ones to get are Symphony, 1,000 grand, Milky Way, Hot Tamales, & Big Hunk. Make your message as short or as long as you like. Brittni adds: if your man is all about that *"fit life"* and today isn't his cheat day, then buy his favorite protein bars and get creative. Some good brands to get are Quest, Cliff, Pure Protein, Zero Impact & One. You can create a love message out of those words. You don't have to be a poet to do it! Just be creative and have fun.

JOURNAL BELOW:

WRITE WHAT YOU LEARNED TODAY, HOW IT
WENT AND WHAT MEMORIES WERE MADE

_____

_____

_____

_____

_____

_____

_____

_____

_____

_____

_____

_____

_____

_____

DAY EIGHTEEN: LET'S GO ON A DATE

To this day, Jeff will still tell you that one of the all-time favorite dates that I took him on was when he came out to Maui to visit me. My youth pastor had let me borrow his truck for the night, so I couldn't wait to take Jeff out somewhere. However, being an intern, I had no money. Like zilch. So I packed a special picnic dinner for us. You know, PB & J's, apples and cookies. I filled up two Nalgene bottles with water and added some crystal light peach packets in them because I knew how much Jeff loved peach flavoring. We drove down the street awhile and then parked where we could back up to the beach. We climbed in the back of the truck, put a blanket down and ate our picnic dinner as we watched the sun sink into the ocean. We talked, laughed and had the best time!

Plan a special date with your guy this week. It doesn't have to be elaborate or expensive, just something intentional that brings you two together. Think of something that he would love to do. It doesn't even have to be that long. If you only can fit in an hour, that's perfect. Some ideas are: have a bonfire, play a board game, chat over a fruit and cheese platter, or go for a romantic evening stroll, and please put your cell phone away, unless it's to snap a quick pic on social media with #31creativeways, so we can see what you did on your date night.

JOURNAL BELOW:

WRITE WHAT YOU LEARNED TODAY, HOW IT WENT AND WHAT MEMORIES WERE MADE

DAY NINETEEN:
DO NOT
DISTURB

Brittni's Insight:

I firmly believe there is nothing more important than spending time with God, especially first thing in the morning. However, this can be challenging with the number of distractions we experience within our generation. The moment we wake up, we have Instagram & facebook alerts, text messages, missed calls, and emails that all need responses on one small device known as the cell phone. When my husband and I were dating, I promised God that my relationship with my boyfriend would never become more of a priority than my relationship with Him. To make this easy on myself, before going to bed, I placed my phone on *"Do Not Disturb."* When my alarm went off in the morning, I woke up, made my tea, then went back to my room to worship, pray and read the Bible. After spending time with God, I would then call my boyfriend. Rich knew that if he called me and I hadn't first sought God, then I wouldn't take his call. I wanted God to know that He could trust me and that I would never leave Him.

In doing so, the following scripture became real in my relationship with Rich. *"Though one may be overpowered, two can defend themselves. A cord of three strands is not quickly broken."* (Ecclesiastes 4:12 NIV)

I love this scripture because it is a reminder that when you and your partner stand firm in God, you form a three-strand cord that cannot be quickly broken. Remember John 10:10 says, *"the thief is out to steal, kill, and destroy"* so we need to be intentional with our devotionals, so the enemy can't destroy the union that God has brought together. When you keep God at the center of your relationship He will become the foundation on which you build on.

If you build on anything other than God it is as though you are building on the sand. The unfortunate thing about this is that when the storms of life hit they are bound to destroy all that was built on sand, because the sand is not a firm foundation. If we eventually want a marriage that lasts a lifetime, then we must build on God who is the rock that will sustain us through the worst of times and through the best of times.

Dating is the perfect time to practice making God your number one priority. In doing so, your life will be beyond blessed. Tonight, put your phone on *"Do Not Disturb"* and when you wake up in the morning, seek God before seeking your boyfriend and social media. As you make this a habit, you'll notice the dynamic of your will change. The two of you will become better and stronger together.

JOURNAL BELOW:

WRITE WHAT YOU LEARNED TODAY, HOW IT WENT AND WHAT MEMORIES WERE MADE

_____

_____

_____

_____

_____

_____

DAY TWENTY: OH, HEY HANDSOME

Laughing is one of my favorite things to do. Tell me a good joke and it'll make my whole day. When I was in junior high, my friend and I use to send each other pick-up lines from this one website. We got the biggest kick out of the ones people came up with and bonus! The website had a new pick up line every day. I always wanted a guy to use one of the pick up lines on me. I mean, how could a girl say no to, *"Looks like you dropped something- my jaw!"*

Today, find a good pick-up line and use it on your guy. Text it, email it, write it in a note. Maybe even have a different one for him every hour! Whatever you do, show him you like him while giving him a good laugh.

JOURNAL BELOW:

WRITE WHAT YOU LEARNED TODAY, HOW IT WENT AND WHAT MEMORIES WERE MADE

_____

_____

_____

_____

_____

_____

_____

DAY TWENTY-ONE: MOVIE NIGHT

Jeff and I love our movie nights. We don't get to the movie theatre much these days, but one of our favorite things to do is pick a good movie on Netflix or Amazon and cuddle up on the couch together. Jeff makes this crazy good popcorn that we put in our special white popcorn bowls and Aslan, our dog, sits by my feet drooling the whole time I chomp away.

Brittni's Insight:

Rich and I love movie nights as well! Movie nights are a great way to get lost in the moment, to forget about the cares in life, and to enjoy quality time with one another. This week, plan a movie night with your man. Bring some snacks, forget about your cares and watch a movie with your man. If you're anything like Rich and I and have a hard time agreeing on a movie, play rock paper scissors. The winner gets to pick the movie!

JOURNAL BELOW:

WRITE WHAT YOU LEARNED TODAY, HOW IT WENT AND WHAT MEMORIES WERE MADE

_____

_____

_____

_____

_____

DAY TWENTY-TWO: THE ART OF THANK YOU

One thing that makes for a successful relationship is found in two words-*"THANK YOU."* Showing that you notice what he's doing and are grateful is monumental in a relationship. It shows that you see him and you appreciate him. Sometimes it can be easy to get caught up in all the things that he's not doing or ways you wish he would change. But that's toxic to a relationship.

When Jeff says thank you to me for doing the things I normally do everyday, it makes me want to keep serving him and gives me joy in the midst of it. Sometimes he'll stop me from what I'm doing, look me in the eye and thank me for something specific. It makes me break out in the biggest smile; it's the best.

This week, focus on saying thank you for the big and little things that your man does. For encouraging you, for opening your car door, for buying you dinner on your dates, and for just being who he is. Today specifically, think of one thing he's done for you and say thank you.

JOURNAL BELOW:

WRITE WHAT YOU LEARNED TODAY, HOW IT WENT AND WHAT MEMORIES WERE MADE

DAY TWENTY-THREE: DRAW A PICTURE

Last weekend we celebrated Kinsley's 2nd birthday. Since Kinsley's favorite thing in the whole world is swimming, we bought her a blow-up pool complete with a slide and ball activities. We had a little pool party with a few of her closest friends. She had a blast! Literally, it was the best day of her life. She giggled and smiled the whole morning. Her friends all brought her a little gift, and all of them included a homemade card. Her friend Ace drew her a stick picture of the two of them together and handed it to her as soon as he saw her. She looked at it, pointed to each stick figure and got the biggest smile on her face.

Cards can sometimes be the best gift of all. I love how little kids draw pictures for people. I have a handful hanging up on my refrigerator right now, displayed as the pieces of artwork that they are.

This may sound silly, but draw a picture of your man today. If you're an incredible artist, then draw something amazing! But if you're like me and stick figures is about as good as it gets, that's OK too! This days action is all about bringing the childlike wonder back into a relationship. It's just something fun and thoughtful. Draw it on a sticky note or construction paper. Draw a picture of your man and point out characteristics he has that you love. Or draw a picture of the two of you together. Maybe draw a picture of when you met, your favorite date or one of your favorite memories. Or draw a picture of something you'd like to do together one day. Whatever it is, I'm sure he'll cherish it as Kinsley cherished her homemade birthday cards.

JOURNAL BELOW:

WRITE WHAT YOU LEARNED TODAY, HOW IT
WENT AND WHAT MEMORIES WERE MADE

_____

_____

_____

_____

_____

_____

_____

_____

_____

_____

_____

_____

_____

_____

DAY TWENTY-FOUR: CHEER-LEADER

I hosted a mom's gathering this last spring with a handful of women who I wanted to get know more. Each week they'd come over for a time of fellowship and learning. An older mom would come and share each week about what they have learned as a mom or wife or what God's taught them over the years. Not only did our group become tight-knit, but we also got to be encouraged by these older women and shaped by their wisdom. One of the ladies who came to teach shared about loving and enjoying her husband. She told us that we as wives are called to be our husbands' biggest cheerleaders. We are to stand by their side, support them, listen well, pray diligently and encourage them. I had known to support and encourage Jeff, but I had never heard it quite phrased that way before, *"be their biggest cheerleader."* I love it that it gives me an awesome picture in my head of one of the main roles as a wife. Even if you're just dating, being a cheerleader for your man is important! Our guys need to know we believe in them and care for them.

Take a picture of yourself today, holding up a sign that says *"GO ___(fill in your man's name)____!"* Send it to him sometime today, letting him know that you are cheering him on!

JOURNAL BELOW:

WRITE WHAT YOU LEARNED TODAY, HOW IT WENT AND WHAT MEMORIES WERE MADE

DAY TWENTY-FIVE: BUCKET LIST

We have these friends who pretty much rock at life. They're some of my favorite people ever and a couple that I look up to. Last year their church focused on loving and pursuing your spouse and encouraged their congregation to go on a date with each other every week. They called it 52 in 15 (2015). As in, 52 dates in 52 weeks. At the end of the year, the couples that did 52 dates were entered into a contest to win a vacation cruise for a week. It's an awesome concept if you ask me! The whole purpose behind it is to encourage married couples to invest in their marriage. Well, this year, our friends are doing it again, but for their dates, they made a bucket list; a list of 52 dates that they want to do with one another. It's been so fun to follow them on Instagram and see the fun dates they do. Some have been making a fruit pizza together, going on a picnic, and making a playlist that reflects their spouse.

Sit down with your guy today or sometime this week and make a bucket list of dates that you want to do together. You don't need to do 52! But get at least ten down that the two of you can do together. Make the bucket list making a little date in itself! Get some yummy snacks, a good drink and have fun scheming together.

JOURNAL BELOW:

WRITE WHAT YOU LEARNED TODAY, HOW IT
WENT AND WHAT MEMORIES WERE MADE

DAY TWENTY-SIX: JUST BECAUSE

"Pleasant words are a honeycomb, sweet to the soul

and healing to the bones."

Proverbs 16:24 (NIV)

Have you ever had someone give you a card or send you a random text that tells you how special you, are and even has a little list of character traits you possess that they love and admire? It's the absolute best. And if you're like me, it usually comes at just the right moment that you need it.

My parents and friends would give me little notes growing up with these sweet sayings, but the one I remember most was an unexpected card from one of my close friends and mentors when I was interning at the church. It had been a long, hard day and to be honest; I was in a season of a lot of growth. Which is a nice way of saying I was a hot mess! The Lord was stretching me and growing me in ways I'd never known was possible. I walked into our office and there on my computer was an envelope with my name beautifully written on the top of it. I opened it up, and there was a list of things she saw in me that were beautiful. Tears stung in my eyes because, amidst all my mess, there was a deep beauty that God was creating and continuing to perfect in me.

Words can make all the difference in someone's day. Send a little text to your man, or give (or mail) him a card today with at least five genuine things that you love about him just because.

JOURNAL BELOW:

WRITE WHAT YOU LEARNED TODAY, HOW IT
WENT AND WHAT MEMORIES WERE MADE

_____

_____

_____

_____

_____

_____

_____

_____

_____

_____

_____

_____

_____

_____

DAY TWENTY-SEVEN: JUST ASK

This past year, Jeff has started to ask me before the day starts or after a heart to heart, what he can do to help me that day? How can he serve me today? And each time that he asks me, my heart softens and calms. Sometimes, I do have some things for him to do that would be helpful to me. But for the most part, it brings me peace and encouragement that he just asks. It shows me that he's thinking of me and reminds me that we're a team. I'm not alone. I don't have to do everything on my own, but he's there to help me in any way. Which, for me, is so encouraging because I tend to get overwhelmed easily.

Ask your guy if there's anything you can do to help him today or this week if you won't see him today. Is there any way you can serve him? Be prepared, if he does have something for you to do and do it cheerfully! But know that just the asking will encourage him too.

JOURNAL BELOW:

WRITE WHAT YOU LEARNED TODAY, HOW IT WENT AND WHAT MEMORIES WERE MADE

_____

_____

_____

_____

_____

DAY TWENTY-EIGHT: ABC

"A,B,C
It's easy as 1,2,3.
As simple as do, re, mi
ABC 1,2,3
Baby, you and me girl."

Today's task will take a little more time and thought, but I promise you it will be something that will bless and honor him.

Pinterest is full of cute little ways to show your man you love him. One year for Valentine's Day I rummaged through a whole list of DIY ideas of things I could make for Jeff. I saw this deck of cards that they punched a hole through on top and put together. On each card, they had written a characteristic trait that they loved about their man. It was so cute! And so I went ahead and whipped (well, not quite!) one up for Jeff. I remember seeing the look on his face when he opened it and read each one. He was so touched that I had spent so much time coming up with 52 things that I love about him. It's still on his side table by his bed as a little reminder that I love him so.

For today's task, I won't ask you to come up with 52 things you love about your man (feel free too though)! However, 26 things seem pretty doable. Get 26 little cards together, 26 sticky notes or just a sheet of paper and write out the ABC's. Come up with a character trait or something that your man does that you love for each letter of the alphabet. It doesn't have to be poetic at all or even artsy. Just dot down 26 things you love about him in alphabetical order.

JOURNAL BELOW:

WRITE WHAT YOU LEARNED TODAY, HOW IT
WENT AND WHAT MEMORIES WERE MADE

_____

_____

_____

_____

_____

_____

_____

_____

_____

_____

_____

_____

_____

_____

DAY TWENTY-NINE: THIS ONE'S ON ME

When Jeff and I first started dating, I thought one of the ways a guy shows you he loves you and is pursuing you is by bringing you your favorite drink from time to time. In all fairness, I did grow up in Seattle, home of the coffee bean. (OK, it's not the home of the coffee bean, but man do we love our coffee there!). So I frequented coffee shops. And if you know me, you know that one of the ways to my heart is by coffee. Straight up, just bring me a cup of coffee with a heavy dose of creamer, and I'll love you forever. Now, Jeff never brought me coffee when we were first dating because of the long distance. The few times we were together, he just didn't know that fact about me because, again, long distance. You just don't know that day in and day out things about the other person because you're never around them. If I'm honest with you, I'll say that this did factor into my breaking up with Jeff the first time. I just didn't think he liked me that much. It's a long story, but man was I wrong. Wrong about Jeff not liking me that much and wrong that true love was summed up in a coffee drink!

I know now true love is about so much more than bringing you your favorite drinks. It's more about faithfulness, kindness, forgiveness, and grace. However, knowing the little ways that show your person you like them and know them is important too and for me, that's coffee. Jeff knows that about me now and will bring me special drinks from time to time. I still remember the second year of marriage, he came home one day with two Starbucks red cups, the first of the season! Talk about TRUE LOVE!

Today, this one's on you. Get your man his favorite drink. Maybe it's coffee like me, or maybe it's a soda, Kombucha or special water. Bring it to him at work, school or pick it up and bring it to him the next time you will see him. He'll love the kind gesture.

JOURNAL BELOW:

WRITE WHAT YOU LEARNED TODAY, HOW IT
WENT AND WHAT MEMORIES WERE MADE

DAY THIRTY: BETTER TO GIVE THAN TO RECEIVE

I'm not gonna lie. I love getting gifts! Not just any gift but ones that are super thoughtful and so me. When I open a gift from someone, and it's exactly what I like, my heart is completely melted because I feel known and loved. It doesn't have to be anything big or expensive (I mean, this girl does love her diamonds, but really...). It can be the smallest thing (and honestly sometimes that's even better) like chocolate in a mason jar because those two things are my love language.

One time I had mentioned to my mom how much I love flowers and so I decided every time I go grocery shopping, I'm just going to buy myself a little bouquet of flowers as a treat to myself. Even if it's just one sunflower, it brings me so much joy to see it every time I walk past it or catch a glimpse of it. Since mentioning my love for flowers to my mom, she has brought me flowers every other week. Now, of course, I didn't tell my mom so she would buy me flowers. But because she is the most thoughtful person in the world, she always thinks of me when she runs into Safeway and will buy me a bouquet because she knows how much they mean to me (I know, she's the best)!

As much as I love receiving gifts, I like giving them even more. I love thinking of a gift that would bless someone I love. The best is when I'm out and about, and I see something that screams one of my friends or family members. I have to get it. Even if it's a "just because" gift.

Gifts don't have to cost much at all; it can be the simplest thing, as long as it says *"I'm thinking of you."* Go out today and get a little something for your man. Maybe it's his favorite candy bar, a pair of his favorite socks, a few guitar picks, a new book that he's been wanting or a couple of movie tickets. Anything that says, *"You are loved and known."*

JOURNAL BELOW:

WRITE WHAT YOU LEARNED TODAY, HOW IT
WENT AND WHAT MEMORIES WERE MADE

_____

_____

_____

_____

_____

_____

_____

_____

_____

_____

_____

_____

_____

_____

DAY THIRTY-ONE: DREAMING TOGETHER

Brittni's Insight:

Rich and I continuously dream on purpose. At the end of every year, we celebrate what we have conquered, and we plan our next moves by writing out our goals. Throughout each year we remind each other of what we are fighting for. A dream, or a vision, makes even the most difficult seasons of life seem so purposeful. Nothing seems like an accident when you have a dream.

Dreaming together as a couple creates a purposeful couple. When you dream together, you no longer make moves just because you have to; you begin to make moves that are directly in alignment with your dream. You begin to understand that to fulfill a dream you must take purposeful steps to get there.

Martin Luther King Jr. changed the course of history because he had a dream. He began to take bold steps that were in alignment with his dream in hopes that his dream would become a reality. Because his steps had a purpose, his dream became a reality.

Imagine what would happen to relationships if we all began to dream on purpose. There is nothing like a couple who is walking with purpose. A couple walking with purpose is unstoppable because they know what they are fighting for and they will not stop until they arrive in a victory.

Proverbs 29:18 says, *"Where there is no vision, the people perish."* This scripture reminds us that having a vision for our lives matters because, without one, we perish. So, if you want your relationship to flourish, then you and you man need a vision for your future together.

Today, have a vision conversation with your man. Talk about your marriage goals, career goals, ministry goals, family goals, what you want to accomplish together and individually, etc. Make sure to journal your goals and dreams, and write out how you plan on reaching them or create a vision board with him! Once you finish, be sure to pray for over your dreams and trust that if God gave you the dream, it will one day become your reality.

JOURNAL BELOW:

WRITE WHAT YOU LEARNED TODAY, HOW IT WENT AND WHAT MEMORIES WERE MADE

_____

_____

_____

_____

_____

_____

_____

_____

_____

DAY THIRTY-TWO: YOUR TURN

You didn't think there was going to be a day 32, did ya? We thought we'd add one more day, to turn it over to you. Think of any idea, any gesture, or any kind thing you can do for your significant other today. Be creative. Be loving. And most of all show them how much you care. Also, we'd love to hear what you picked for day 32! We might even end up including it in future versions or volumes of this book. You can upload your idea at 31creativeways.com/upload. We can't wait to hear how creative you guys are and what y'all came up with!

JOURNAL BELOW:

WRITE DOWN ANY IDEA, GESTURE OR KIND THING YOU CAN DO FOR YOUR SIGNIFICANT OTHER

_____

_____

_____

_____

_____

_____

A NOTE FROM US AFTER FINISHING THIS BOOK

First off, you all rock! For reals. Complete rockstars. Why? Because you care about your relationship. You're investing in it. You believe in it. It matters to you.

We believe that a relationship is like a garden. For it to flourish, it needs proper nourishment, constant care, awareness of the things trying to hurt it and sometimes is a little messy. This book is just a start to hopefully continuing or taking that leap of putting you and your significant other on the path to a vibrant and beautiful relationship.

So thank you for doing this journey with us. Thank you for reading this book. And thank you for just being you. We'd love to hear from you and how the challenge went by sharing something online with the hashtag #31creativeways. We are constantly on that hashtag to see all the awesome stuff you guys are doing, ways you tweaked one of our challenges to make it better and to see all the fun you're having!

For those who maybe are getting this as a gift or don't know much about us, below are just a few other things we have created and done over the past few years. **We hope they encourage you!**

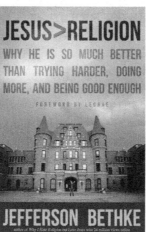

Find at
JEFFBETHKE.COM

Find at
BETHKEWORKSHOPS.COM

WHERE TO FIND US ONLINE

We love when folks give us a shout on social media, so feel free to stop by and say hey! Would love to E-meet you.

INSTAGRAM

@jeffersonbethke
@alyssajoybethke

TWITTER

@jeffersonbethke
@alyssajoybethke

FACEBOOK

fb.com/jeffersonbethkepage
fb.com/alyssajoybethke

SNAPCHAT
Username: jeffersonbethke

WEBSITES

jeffandalyssa.com
alyssajoy.me
bethkeworkshops.com
31creativeways.com

We are always looking for great things to help marriages and relationships. We've found a few we absolutely love and hope you guys will too!

DATEBOX:

We LOVE this. It's a subscription service that sends you a fully curated Datebox every month to your doorstep. For example, during the Christmas season in December we got a box that included a gingerbread making kit, two custom mugs, hot cocoa mix, a Christmas playlist and bunch more goodies. We have a blast every time one shows up on our door. We wanted to hook you guys up to check it out. If you use code 'bethke' at checkout at **http://www.getdatebox.com**, you get your first month 50% off. Definitely a steal of a deal and something we love!

Strongermarriages.com: This is a phenomenal website that has crazy amounts of content to help and build any marriage out there! They have courses, blogs, books and more. It's a site that isn't afraid to talk about real life either, which is so important to us.

Made in the USA
Coppell, TX
17 May 2020